Peeking into my Garden

Marylou Kalb Constantino

Parson's Porch Books

Peeking into my Garden
ISBN: Softcover 978-1-949888-53-9
Copyright © 2016 by Marylou Kalb Constantino

All rights reserved. No part of this book may be reproduced or transmitted in any form or by any means, electronic or mechanical, including photocopying, recording, or by any information storage and retrieval system, without permission in writing from the publisher.

To order additional copies of this book, contact:

Parson's Porch Books
1-423-475-7308
www.parsonsporch.com

Parson's Porch Books is an imprint of Parson's Porch & Company (PP&C) in Cleveland, Tennessee. PP&C is an innovative company which raises money by publishing books of noted authors, representing all genres. All donations from contributors and profits from publishing are shared with the poor.

Peeking into my Garden

Acknowledgments

Front Cover Illustration by Joan Marie Caswell, Artist, Blairsville, Georgia

Dedication Photo by Patricia Smith Browning, Annapolis, Maryland

My Grandchildren by Stacy Janette Constantino, JC's Story Teller Photography, San Antonio, Texas

Foreword by Charlotte Barr - Poetess Emetrius

Pam Diane's Portrait by Hollywood Studios, Baltimore, Maryland

Frank Constantino, Jr, and his dog, Henry by Marylou Constantino

The Depth of Our Love, by Marylou Constantino, published on legacy.com/William J. Toner

Back Cover Photo by Olan Mills Photography, Baltimore, Maryland

Dedication

This book is dedicated to my husband of 47 years, Frank Ho'opai Constantino, who has been my constant companion and now caregiver and to my high school friend of 65 years, Joan Marie Caswell, artist, who walked beside me in the garden. Both have peeked into my past and helped me survive. I love and respect you both.

I cannot forget my forever friends who have blessed me with their friendship in so many ways, Kim Atma, Charlotte Barr - Poetess Emeritus, Natalie Blakely, Patricia Browning "my adopted daughter" Judith Fishburne, Susan Santiago, Loretta Wilbanks and my Hawaiian Ohana (Family) too numerous to mention by name. You live in my heart.

Easter with My Grandchildren

I have been blessed with five grandchildren:

Ryan Christopher Hurley (missing from photo)
Christopher Jordan Hurley
Ethan Darwin Constantino
Audrey Melia Constantino
Avery Diego Constantino

Table of Contents

A Peek into my Garden	15
A Glimpse of My Memories	16
Sea Voyage	17
A Toast to Ron	18
April Fool	19
Army Wife	21
Autumn	22
Banjo Country	23
Beloved Spirit	24
First Grade	25
God sent me a Daughter	27
Guard Duty	28
Haiku	29
Heaven Gained	30
I Wonder	31
Just Because	32
Life	33
Love	34
Magic Sands	35
Mama's Look	36
Mary's Law	37
How not to wash a cell phone	38

My Companion	39
My Son	40
Needs	42
Open Hearts	43
Passion	44
Prelude to Divorce	45
Reunited	46
Save the Animals	47
Teeny Tiny	48
The Depth of Love	49
The End	50
The Last Supper	51
To Theresa	52
Traveling Memories	53
Triumph Tulip	54
What goes around	55
When I die	56
Winning a Scrabble Game	57
Woe	58

Epigraph

This book will show both sides of my life from early childhood to the current year. The poems and prose were written at different periods, and I hope that I have given an insight to both the good times and bad. I believe happiness overcomes evil, and I pray that the reader will agree. I am 79 years old and now able to put these years on paper. Read with me and enjoy or weep.

During counseling sessions, I was advised that "The Devil was at my heels" and amazingly, I was still alive.

No one seemed to be aware of child abuse and I suffered alone. It took many years before I realized the cause of my emotional pain. My parents did not know. I remember asking my sister if she had any idea of what was going on in my life and she said no and if she had known she would have killed my abuser. I love her for that. My family is gone now, leaving me the Matriarch with two adult children and five grandchildren. God has helped on the way, and I am a survivor. My prayer is that everyone be aware of the effects child abuse has on the soul and all aspects of the abused's life.

Foreword

Mary Constantino's collection of poems. *Peeking into My Garden,* both hides and reveals a lifetime of pleasure and pain, decades of joy and sorrow. It offers a peek, that is all. But to those who know this warm yet reticent woman—and perhaps to those who will know her only through her verse it is enough. We must walk carefully through her garden: the flowers are delicate; the scents and colors seem muted to the casual visitor. But there is vibrancy and verve just under the surface that leaps out, "shining like shook foil" that both startle and satisfy the visitor who has the patience and perception to touch without bruising the flowers that grow there: the buried memories and subtle recollections of a long life fully lived. In Mary's plot of earth, to borrow from the poet Hopkins once again, "There lives the dearest freshness deep down things" (God's Grandeur).

Yet not all is sweetness and light. There are shadows and secrets too. I can hear the whisper of that desperate prayer from one of the poet-priest's 'Terrible Sonnets": "Mine, O thou lord of life, send my roots rain" (Gerard Manley Hopkins, 'Thou Art Indeed Just, Lord"). Just as her "Triumph Tulip" knows that "The chill of winter prepares me for birth." Mary knows, as only a mother knows, that pain is the price of birth and as only a child robbed of innocence can know "The childhood lost will never heal" (Woe).

These poems are both simple and profound, as is the life they reflect. Mrs. Constantino gives us a glimpse of that crucible where all souls are shaped: the family, where all the drama begins and only ends with the final curtain. Her parents, siblings, Catholic school "Wearing an ugly blue uniform with scratchy white collar, husbands, children, grandchildren, a beloved nephew gone too soon, a baby lost and another gained, friends, foes, dogs, travels, work, youth, sickness, age, and abiding faith are all here, in hints and guesses, prayers, and reveries. Poets never tell the whole story.

What is not said is often the deepest truth. As Mary writes, "Life is full, yet life is small." She understands the mystery and the paradox that life is made of and that poetry tries to express.

Inside myself are bows of joy when gently untied,
Release all the love I've tucked inside (Just Because).

In one poem, the speaker is a banjo, in another a ship. In all of these poems, the author plays hide and seek; she is in the words and disguised by them. Mary Constantino's shyness and openness are woven throughout, but never more artfully and gracefully than in her spare yet redolent "Haiku":

The rain will suddenly cease
When the heavens tire of crying tears
All creatures will scamper gloriously

Here is a garden of verse from my friend and fellow-poet that is worth more than a peek, dear reader. Enter and enjoy.

Charlotte Barr
10 August 2016

A Peek into My Garden

Peek in my garden and what will you see?
A glimpse of childhood misery.
Please look very closely at those tears.
Later you may find happiness in later years.

I was a gentle flower in my early life,
Whose petals were torn apart by strife.
Abused and tattered deep inside,
Somehow the blossom stayed alive.

There was much sorrow through years of pain.
It took almost a lifetime to find myself again.
I'm happy to have weathered my storms quite well
By writing my poems, my story I tell.

A Glimpse of My Memories

Why does the past come to see me?
Why does it knock on my door?
Will it ever relieve me?
And let me live free once more?

Can't I blank out my mind of old memories?
I tried it, it happened one day, then
Peace and security surrounded me
And in happiness, I lived every day.

Now it comes back with pain and sorrow
To bare my soul and harass me
To plague and rip me to shreds.
So I'll live for today and tomorrow
And wonder each day what's ahead.

A Sea Voyage

I am a ship moving slowly,
So slowly through the sea,
I look at my hull and see that I am
Covered with barnacles
Dragging me slowly over the brine.
How long have they been attached to me?
Why are they there?
Yearly, I go to dry dock for maintenance
But the pesky creatures always return
Slowing me down in my life's voyage
Be gone barnacles!
You are not wanted or needed.
I control my own destiny
I take the helm
Suddenly I am free and moving swiftly
Through the current of life
Sailing the oceans contently
Climbing the mask, aware of sea grass,
And looking back no more.

A Toast to Ron

First my neighbor, then my friend
A "Good Ole Guy"
Though he did not flaunt it,
Married to Sally, my friend, the poet

His handlebar mustache from side to side,
Was it for fun or for disguise?
Always a gentleman, kind, helping and wise
Too soon gone, no time for goodbyes.

He lives in our minds,
His spirit now free,
In thoughts, he will always be
Remembered with love eternally.

April Fool

April Fool, April Fool
What a funny thing to say
If I hear it again
I will run the other way
January Fool, January Fool
Snow is beginning to lay
The weather's frosty and cool
On a bright and snowy day
February Fool, February Fool
May think he's in love
And knows not what to do
Please Cupid, give him a shove
Tell him to bring flowers and a Valentine too
March Fool, March Fool.
Being blown along the street
Howling winds and the Ides of March
Might knock him off his feet
May Fool, May Fool
Spring and blossoms in the air
Are sure to bring a smile
Seeing daffodils everywhere
Planting a garden is never a trial
June Fool, June Fool,
Fishing and boating, always in tune
Swimming and picnics not to be missed
Weddings are very important in June
With so many brides waiting to be kissed
July Fool, July Fool
It's hot and muggy but summer's here
Have fun, relax and have a cool drink
Enjoy each minute, no need to fear
Cooler weather will be here in a wink
August Fool, August Fool
School's about to begin
Some children are very sad

While others will grin
Many will dress in the latest fad
September Fool, September Fool
The air is cooler and brings delight
Labor Day is a holiday celebrated
Both day and night
The end of a season perhaps overrated
October Fool, October Fool
Witches and goblins will knock on the door
It's Fall and Halloween is near
Buying lots of treats is never a chore
When vampires and monsters suddenly appear
November Fool, November Fool
Mashed potatoes, gravy, cranberry sauce
Friends, relatives are invited to eat
Get the turkey ready whatever the cost
Mom will be in the kitchen on her feet
December Fool, December Fool
Santa's coming soon.
It's time to enjoy
Don't forget to praise
The Savior, God's Little Boy
The year is over
I don't want it to go
But another one's coming
Right after the snow!

Army Wife

The soldier's wife lives all alone.
She's a fortress by herself,
She tries to keep the children fed.
Her emotions on a shelf.
And when the house starts tumbling down
And troubles are at her door.
She firmly fights her battles and loves her soldier more.

She loves her little children and helps them grow up strong.
Focusing her attention, teaching them right from wrong.
She deserves a special medal for service above the call,
Very few could fill her shoes, she's always on the ball.
So give a lot of credit to the lady of the nest,
She's definitely a winner and a step above the rest!

Autumn

Spring and Summer are memories now
I walk, breath and feel the leaves change
Saffron and russet beauties fall covering my footsteps
My canine companion isn't concerned with the hues of Fall
He keenly scans for log-hopping bunnies
And squirrels gleaning acorns for Winter
Rapidly he darts ahead
Then stops with attentive ears perked
Looks back to ensure I am not lost
He'll wait awhile then race to beat me home
No human would know we had been here
The trees and birds look down and know
Waiting patiently for tomorrow
When we will walk Autumn's path again

Banjo Country

If I were a banjo, I'd live in the mountains
Surrounded by wildflowers, frogs and
such
Sometime sad but never too much
My music would sing from a rickety porch

My days are content just knowing I'll be
Sprouting melodious sounds with happy memories
My listeners slapping their knees with a bang
While I'm picking and strumming with twinkle and twang

Children would start singing old country songs
While carefree and dancing, knowing they belong
I see there's a little girl all dressed up in lace
She's beautiful and shines with a glowing inner grace

Making hearts joyful is never a chore
A fiddle and I join as never before
We continue until it seems like a race
I'm exhausted then happily return to my case.

Beloved Spirit

By the honeysuckle breathed a creature
Who by appearance had indefinite feature
As never before, I stood surprised
Now that the blossoms have gone away
I see him in the bright of day
His proud spirit is here to stay.

First Grade

Oh Boy! Do I remember grammar school?
Legless women floating around in long, black, serge skirts.
Children dodging huge swinging rosaries while
Wearing ugly blue uniforms with scratchy white collars.

I know it's called school but what is this place'?
What was my Mom thinking sending me here?
Does she want me to suffer
Wearing an ugly blue uniform with a scratchy white collar?

Hooray! Recess finds me in the schoolyard corner afraid to join
The many small creatures jumping and screaming in play.
Creatures almost exactly like me
Wearing ugly blue uniforms with scratchy white collars.

I hear the gigantic school bell gonging.
Calling all inside to find what our captor plans for us
The rest of this day in a dreary, dark room.
Wearing ugly blue uniforms with scratchy white collars.

Someone gets their knuckles cracked for whispering.
Another one winds up in the cloak room for chewing gum.
What is a cloak room? Will they actually put us in a cloak,
Wearing ugly blue uniforms with scratchy white collars?

I struggle to keep my eyes from welling with tears.
Will I do something wrong and get whacked with a ruler?
I sneak a glance at the lumpy girl in a desk beside me
Wearing an ugly blue uniform with a scratchy white collar.

Ding Dong! Lunch time in the damp basement cafeteria where
No lunch is served. Are you joking?
Not even a respectable mouse would eat here
Wearing an ugly blue uniform with a scratchy white collar.

My square lunch box with it's wax paper wrapped sandwich,
Looks shabby as I see Mary Ann next to me, open hers,
Inside are dainty little carrot sticks which she relishes
Wearing an ugly blue uniform with a scratchy white collar.

After noon we are ushered back to the classroom by
These no-legged women who dare us to breathe.
Chalk screeches across the blackboard; we copy our homework
Wearing ugly blue uniforms with scratchy white collars.

BRRRRRing!! Is that a fire alarm?
No! It's time to catch the bus for the ride home.
I will be happy to see my Mom. Will I have to return tomorrow
Wearing this ugly blue uniform with a scratchy white collar?

Today, I'm amazed as I remember these mean-looking women, young
    arid old.
They didn't despise us. They managed to organize, teach, discipline
And direct us in single file to the right buses while
Wearing their long, black, serge garments and swinging rosaries.
Then they smiled!

God sent me a Daughter

God looked on a teenager who was confused and sad
And sent me the best gift from Heaven He had.
My little girl, princess of my heart
A peachy complexion and joy from the start.
Bright, shiny eyes, I gazed into with love
Thanking God in heaven above,
All babies are beautiful but you were the best
Because you were mine and better than the rest.
Your precious, little smile and perfect button nose
Perfect from your head down to your twinkle-toes.
Your beauty and innocence but a touch of your charm
I pray God will protect you and keep you from harm.

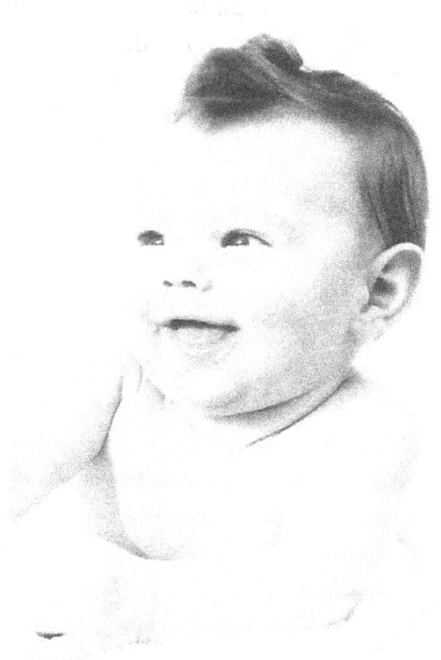

Guard Duty

Standing guard duty is never any fun,
You're praying that an inmate will not decide to run,
Working in a tower can really drive you crazy,
This job is so sad that it really makes you lazy,
Monotony drives yourself insane, finding things to do,
Then the stupid clock says, your shift is only half way through
You're talking on the telephone, playing with your gun,
Listening to the radio, sitting on your bun,
You ate your whole lunch about an hour ago or two,
And now the doggone munchies start to get to you,
You're chewing on your fingernails, looking for some gum,
Dreaming of a pizza, felling really glum,
You know you're going nuts and it's much more than a hunch,
When you plot to kill the guy in tower five, just to steal his lunch
You're sure time's stopped, your panic starts to swell,
You're on the edge of madness, you're sliding into hell,
But wait, you can't believe your eyes, your relief is now in sight,
In your heart, you're still depressed, you'll be back
tomorrow... right?

Haiku

The rain will suddenly cease
When the heavens tire of crying tears
All creatures will scamper gloriously

Heaven Gained

A tiny baby thrust into life so innocent and pure
Not knowing what awaits through an evil doer
It said that humans plan their own future and fate
Not so when a devil incarnate enters the gate
Forced to drink sin at a very young age
Far better to have been fettered, jailed in a cage
No one to the rescue, no one to confide
A childhood confusing, one hell of a ride
Torture never ending, cemented in the heart
The scars still remain and never depart
A little mind battered, grown up to be scorned
No time for lost years or laughter mourned
Dwelling on pain does not bring relief
Masking the shame will not end the grief
The monster that abused the body and soul
Though now deceased, left a festering hole
Good Bye, Mr. Sam Reid, you caused so much pain
Forgiving was difficult but brought Heaven's gain

I Wonder

The love of my youth has passed away
Where is he today?
I wonder…

Could he be around me now?
Does he know just how?
I wonder…

I think of him once in awhile
And would he smile?
I wonder…

By remembering romantic days before
Am I keeping him from Eternity's door?
I wonder…

I wonder…
Where I would be
If I were dead instead of he!

Just Because

Inside myself are bows of joy when gently untied,
Release all the romance I've tucked inside.
Just because I love you, perhaps I should tell you why,
You are important to me and my special guy.

Just because I love you says many things for me.
It's why I want you, Darling, with me constantly.
And also it's the reason when you are around,
Pleasure lifts my very being swiftly off the ground.

If, just because I love you, makes me feel this way,
Then you fulfill my life today and every day.
When I give myself to you and remain yours true,
What other answer is there, than because I love just you.

Life

Life is full of joy, Behold!
A little child, a story told,
A blossom rare, a gem divine,
The sun, the moon and stars are mine.

Life is full, yet life is small!
A path paved for one and all,
Yet, when you love as did I,
What is left, but to die?
He's gone, there's but an empty shelf,
All alone, me and myself.

Life is full of woe, Alas!
A wound, an ache too deep to pass,
Death, sin and Satan's gate,
Leave thoughts on which to dwell and hate.

Life is full of sorrow, no rest!
Would that I die and unburden my breast,
Be there such peace, reward me today,
Grant me eternity forever to stay.
My life is done, my deeds in store,
Would that I die and breathe no more.

Love

Define it, if you can,
Conquer it, I dare thee, man,
Abuse it and if you try,
Life's most precious gift will die.

Cherish it, so you desire,
Guard it, as you admire,
Protect it, as I do mine,
And life's most precious gift is thine.

Magic Sands Beach

The surf and sand of Hawaii's Magic Beach
Disappear for months and return
In Summer like homing pigeons
Waiting to grab wading toes.

Unaware of rocky terrain, jelly fish, shells
Tiny toes hiding below the brine.
Cover themselves in silky grains
And dig in for balance.

A foamy wave grabs the sand and
Sweeping toes and body upside down.
An adrenal rush energizes them
Toes tumbling with fear and excitement.

Suddenly, regaining their composure,
Saved and unaware of salvation.
They look to tomorrow,
Another day at Magic Sands!

Mama's Look

Mama never spanked me
She didn't have to,
Because when she gave me "That Look"
I knew what I should do!

She surveyed my games with pleasure
And then would come the frown
When I overstepped my limits
And acted like a clown!

I'll admit that look was scary
It could stop me in my tracks
It even worked on Papa
When Mama wanted facts.

It worked from crib to teenager
And even in my prime
I'll remember that look Mama gave
Kept me from all crime!

Now, Mama's a senior citizen
She smiles approval all day long
Oh! How I miss her love and look she gave
That showed me right from wrong!

Mary's Law

The dogs have fleas.
I burned my arm.
It's raining outside.
I'm in a state of alarm.

The car won't start.
IRS sent me a letter.
I lost my keys.
It's got to get better.

I spilled my coffee.
My day's been bad.
Could it get worse?
Of course, it could…
I could be in a hearse.

How not to wash a cell phone

My cell phone died. I wondered why?
It had a soapy bath in the washer,
A spin and tumble in the dryer then,
Magically appearing clean and dry.
No sound, no sigh or peep is uttered.
Was the sudsy adventure fun?
Did names and numbers call out for rescue?
Did they relax and enjoy the bath?
What a sad sight!
Unable to text, call, or answer.
Off I go to the phone store,
Feeling remorseful and contrite.
I vow to protect my new phone by
Always searching all pockets
Oh No! There was a hiding place in my blouse,
And now I find myself washing clothes by hand!

My Companion

My poetry book, my constant friend
My Companion from day start to end
You offer your pleasures with me to share
And my soul release from worry and care.

Your treasures take me many places
And introduce numerous facts and faces
For me to spend time reading with delight
Good grief, I hope we never fight!

My Son - Frank D. Constantino

Your baby died, the doctor said
The facts were cold and bare
I never held him to my breast
Or touched his baby hair.
Why did he die? I asked myself,
As I gazed about the room,
And struggled in my head with
Sorrowful thoughts of gloom.
Six years went by without my son
Then my soul was filled with joy
The Agency called me up and said,
Come pick up your boy.
He was such a tiny tot,
A little lad of three
And when I held him in my arms,
He became a part of me.
As years went by and he grew up
My heart never questioned why,
One little boy lived with me and
Another had to die.
The years flew by and now he's grown
This young man, I call my own,
Someday he'll realize how much he's meant to me,
Filling the void within my soul, exchanging it with glee.
He's good and kind and wonderful,
A fighter for our country, ensuring that we are free
Thank you, God, for every day
He spent his life with me.

Needs

Woman needs man to stay young and gay
Man needs woman each and every day
Both need baby to brighten the way
Families need love to keep troubles away
All need to hope and also to say
Please God, fill our needs, we pray.

Open Hearts
In memory of
Mary Catherine Kalb
1907-1985

Our hearts open up and we see you there
Your smile, your love is everywhere
Surrounding us with peace
We know you are at rest,
That the angels came and took the best.
Life is a moment in our journey to be
Perfect and kind to all that we see
You did all that and so much more
We will meet again, Mom, at Heaven's Door.

Passion

My love for you is misunderstood
My love for you under purity's hood
Burns with a fire as kindled by wood.

I give my heart because I love you, dear
Cherish it and keep it very near
Left alone, it will perish, I fear.

My passion is alive and fragile you see
Living for your love is vital to me
You alone hold my future's key.

Prelude to Divorce

Alone in our thoughts
Together in bed
Much on our minds
But not a word said
Declarations of love
Are meaningless now
Words can't be spoken
And would end up foul
A question, an answer
Always twisted around
Make each feel useless
And brought to the ground
What is the remedy?
Can the heartache end?
We cannot tell anyone
Certainly not a friend
One is always sorry
For saying a word
Which causes hurt and anger
Better seen and not heard
We are losing our footing
And not having a say
Interferes with the opinion
Of the other every day
Everything seems one way
No one wants to lose control
So we live underground
Much like a mole
The day will be soon
When it comes to a head
We'll decide divorce is better
Than staying wed.

Reunited
A Memorial
William Joseph Toner
1972 - 2012

You will always be 40,
That's when you left this life.
Your Mom never knew your struggle.
Your Dad never knew your strife.
If only they had known your agony and pain,
They'd have showered you with kisses again, and again.
No one knows their heartbreak, no one feels their grief.
Knowing your suffering is over doesn't bring them relief,
Everyone wonders wherein lies the blame.
And living life without you will never be the same.
When we all go to Heaven, what a joyous reunion it will be.
We will all be whole again, a reunited family.

Save the animals

"Save the animals," God shouts from above
Looking down and showering His love
They are all beautiful and precious in His sight
He wants us to be aware of their plight
He gave them to us to teach man kindness
Wondering why so many show blindness
To their fear, sadness and longing for care
What can God do to make man aware?
He could take the dogs, cats and farm creatures away
Remove the deer from the forest and fish from the bay
So show compassion, feed the hungry, give comfort to those
Out in bad weather, and don't you suppose
That giving them a safe, warm space
Would put a smile on God's face?

Teeny Tiny: A Dog

A gift for my daughter who wanted a horse.
So this little dog was rejected, of course.
He chewed up her dress, we didn't know why.
But Houdini had nothing on this little guy.

He chased away boyfriends, was terror of the house.
Caused a lot of turmoil, no bigger than a mouse.
I adopted him and named him Teeny Tiny.
He was sweet to me but occasionally whiny.

Rode in the car with the splendor of Tut
No one dared to call him a mutt.
Unwinding toilet paper was his favorite pastime.
He feigned innocence all through his prime.

Loved by me and hated by the rest
I have to admit he was sometimes a pest.
He wasn't afraid of anything in sight.
Bullied people around with all of his might.

He was little and mean but loved me so much.
Protected me always, how I miss his touch.
This little dog hated being alone.
When left by himself, chewed furniture like a bone.

He gnawed on men's pants legs and put me in a spot.
Trying to explain why the pants were shredded a lot
Tiny loved hiding under a chair or a couch.
And biting everyone's legs till they screamed "ouch"

He roamed the back yard looking for game.
Many a rabbit trembled at his name.
There have been many others, but I loved him so much.
That none can replace his snuggling touch.

The depth of our love

It seems you arrived on angel wings
And stayed long enough to teach us things
Things like gentility, kindness and most of all, love
Then you were called back to Heaven above

So, we had you and your goodness for a little while
We will cherish the days that you made us smile
Having you in our lives was truly a treasure
The pain we now feel is without measure

Our hearts are broken and empty today
But we know your spirit is with us to stay
So visit us often in our lives every day
And at night in our dreams, be near where we lay
For no one can ever replace you, B.J.

I wrote this poem for my darling nephew.
Published on Legacy.com/WilliamJToner

The End

Writing furiously now, for time is not my friend
So much to do, I'll be working to the end

Getting things in order, must not leave a mess
Donating many items, including my wedding dress

Many things once precious I'll leave behind
The joyful days, I've wined and dined

I live in pain and hope to die
As the days go quickly and continuously by

Friends I've loved, who loved me well
Those who didn't can go to hell

Not many will mourn, not many will cry
I gave them all my love and know not why

I cling to the religion of my youth
Saturdays spent in the confessional booth

Memories of a communion day
With garlands of flowers and songs of May

Learning Latin and singing in church choirs
Too late now to complete my desires

Things I've collected, treasures to me
An Estate Sale will take some, the rest will be free

Who will get my crystal and gold?
Everyone wants them so I'm told

Let everyone fight, I do not care
Where were they when I needed them there?

The Last Supper
In Memory of
Louis Charles Kalb
1900 – 1976

As I near my eighties, I see you in your wonder years
Always happy, with a smile on your face
Your seventy five years on Earth now seem so few
A lone survivor of three infant siblings, Florence,
Charles, Edward and the 1904 Baltimore fire
Elder brother of Daniel, Thomas, Marie and Agnes Garvey
A member of the Maryland National Guard and Knights of Columbus
Smoking took you from me as it has done so many others
I was always afraid of your booming voice and
Hid under the bed when you came home from work
Your child remembers you performing in a Minstrel Show
Confused to see you in a black face singing and dancing
Waademeloms, red waademelons, you sang,
That you didn't know where you were going when you died,
But you crooned, if there were a lot of waademelons over there,
That would be Heaven to you, yes sir, that would be heaven to you.
You sired two daughters, were you disappointed one wasn't a son
To carry on your Germanic name of which you were so proud?
How happy if you had known Baron De Kalb, your ancestoral soldier
Sailing over the Atlantic, fighting, bravely giving his life
In Washington's Army of the Potomac for our freedom
I can see you embracing him in the clouds at a Heavenly Gasthaus
You joked about the accident that robbed you of your eye
Did it make you stronger or help to mask your suffering and pain?
You were so brave and didn't tell of the cancer that took you
Was it so horrible that you couldn't tell? You shielded us from knowing.
You protected us during World War II as an Air Raid Warden
You were a courageous soldier and never once complained
We buried you in my grave in The Last Supper Garden
Too late now, the door is closed and yet
I long to find out more about you
To put your tears, smiles, and laughter here.

To Theresa

My sister is the nicest person I have ever seen.
She was always sweet and kind and never, never mean!
She never threw her shoe at me, the baby of the nest,
Although I know within her mind.
I'm fondly called the pest.
I love her though, with all my heart
Believe it or not,
Even though when I was a kid.
She kicked me around a lot!
Sometimes, I think she loves me too,
For when she screams and shouts,
She says it in her fondest voice,
"Get out, you brat, Get out!"

Traveling Memories

Seeing the sights of my dreams
Still asleep, sometimes, it seems

Remembering these places, never a chore
Make staying at home somewhat less of a bore

Hawaii, Alaska, Europe and Caribbean in living color
Make Home Sweet Home just a tiny bit duller

Driving in Mexico, Germany, Switzerland, Holland and France
Put this adventurous traveler into a trance

The windmills and tulips in Holland, amazing to the eye
God created this world, how could anyone wonder why?

Evening in a Gasthaus drinking Moselle wine
Savoring strong coffee in Ider Oberstein

Cruising the Rhine and walking Heidelberg's steps
Took all of my energy, vigor and pep

Excitedly viewing the Alps from a cable car
And watching Madam Pele's magnificent fury from afar

Swimming in the Caribbean Sea near Coakley Bay
Sailing to Buck Island and snorkeling all day

Seeing Alaska's wilderness and making a forever friend
What more could I ask? So my traveling is at an end.

Triumph Tulip

I live underground and like it.
How old am I? Not very.
In fact, I just arrived last fall.
The chill of winter prepares me for birth.

Feeling the warmth of the springtime, now
I open my eyes. I have lots of friends:
A rose, anemone, jonquil, iris.
But my pink and yellow petals are best!

A neighbor admires us as she looks out her window.
Every day she talks to us.
If I had a pretty vase, I would plop myself on her window sill.
But I must be content with spreading beauty outside.

You may call me Wonder Woman Flower.
I promise to share my beauty again,
Isn't that a Wonder?
Next Spring I'll sprout and put other blossoms to shame.

Tulips reign!

What goes around...

Bullies don't know what they do to the heart
Ripping and shredding and tearing apart.
Innocent victims unaware that they are
Moments away from leaving childhood afar.

Tormentors taunt, ridicule, tear at the soul
Of another who simply had one goal.
To be accepted and chosen on a team to play
Difference, size or looks kept them away.

Offenders are happy, it makes them feel bold
To leave another out in the cold.
Their cruel words and actions carelessly spoken
Crush young spirits and leave them broken.

The wounds don't heal, are carried through life
Pain never eases and cuts like a knife.
Feeling this torture, years later. . . today
Makes living life difficult each day.

Wanting acceptance, eager to please
Does not manage to erase and ease.
So Bullies be mindful of the pleasure you feel
For karma will come to you in life's rotating wheel.

When I die...

The world will not know it
There will be no headlines
No fanfare, no memorials
Not many will mourn nor care

I may leave crying as when I was birthed
On a Wednesday evening in the Spring
Or perhaps I'll be smiling to finally see
The mystery of the other side

People who have loved me may be there
To greet me and eagerly show me around
They may forgive my mistakes and let me know
I wasn't so bad, just a human being

They will know I was one who loved from the heart
Made errors in judgment and paid the price
On Earth and leaving all behind maybe then I will find
True happiness

Winning a Scrabble Game

Enjoying a game of Scrabble
Small wooden squares
Floating around in space
Seeking a place to land
Unable to move when placed.

Silently waiting for a companion
To attach which, unhappily
Achieves a higher score
Discouraged not, but determined
To play another game, another day
I lost, but next time I may win.

So, these important square tiles
Fusing in my brain
Inviting magical words
Linked together by my mind
Connected numbers into an unbeatable score.
I win!

Woe

Life is not all fun and games, we see for many years.
We learn the hard way through heartaches and tears.
Once I faced life filled with joy and spirits high,
Since then, I found man had one destiny, that is but to die.

Woe awaits those full of whim,
Pain awaits the fool,
Eternity awaits all, for man is but a tool,
To die a little every day seems to be our fate
Actions and words hurt deeply when brimmed with hate.

To carry on and try to be brave
Holding secrets unto the grave
Is a great burden to bear
It tears at the heart which ceases to care.

Mistakes are made because of the past
Memories of abuse unceasingly last
Perhaps peace will come in the night
When Heaven is reached and I enter the light.

The pain that is suffered is always real
The childhood lost will never heal
So protect little children and mind what you do
For the torture they feel is inflicted anew.

About the Author

Marylou Kalb Constantino

In 1937, I was born into a family who loved each other, parties and song. So I quickly learned all of the drinking songs of the 20's, 30's and 40's. My parents grew up during the Depression and Flapper era so after that life was good for them. I love my parents. I was raised as a Roman Catholic and attended Catholic schools for 12 years. My parents didn't attend church because they had both been married previously and divorced, so I went to Mass with neighbors. Later, they reconciled with the church. I was very proud of the fact that I was in the choir and could sing the Mass in Latin. The English language was my first love and Latin wasn't far behind.

In the 50's, women had few choices: Catholic girls either married, entered a convent or went to college. With no funds for college, rejected by the convent because I came from divorced parents, I chose marriage to another Catholic which pleased my parents very much. Looking back, I see that I was always pleasing everyone except myself. Anyway, marriage it was, followed by childbirth, divorce and remarriage.

I was a journalist for the Seton High School newspaper and I was hooked on writing and started writing poems in 1954. My essay was published in the National Anthology of High School Students in 1955 and I wrote the Border Patrol Miami Sector newsletter in 1991. After my second marriage, I attended college whenever I could afford a class or two and graduated from Park College, Parkville, Missouri, with a degree in Criminal Justice in 1989. As an Army wife, I lived and traveled through Germany, Switzerland, France and Holland. I have lived and worked in law enforcement in Oklahoma, Kansas, Miami, Texas, Hawaii, and the U.S. Virgin Islands. I started working at age 16 and eventually retired from The Department of Justice in 2002.

This book is a collection of the bits and pieces of my mind and the flowers and weeds in my garden.

www.ingramcontent.com/pod-product-compliance
Lightning Source LLC
Chambersburg PA
CBHW052208110526
44591CB00012B/2125